MEDITATION
GATEWAY TO LIGHT

by

ELSIE SECHRIST

A·R·E PRESS

ASSOCIATION FOR
RESEARCH AND
ENLIGHTENMENT

SELF DISCIPLINE

Q. How can I discipline myself . . . to do what is mine to do?

A. Repeat three times every day, and then listen: "LORD, WHAT WOULD THOU HAVE ME DO TODAY?" Have this not as rote. Mean it! For as He has spoken, as He has promised, 'If ye call, I will hear and answer speedily.' He meant it! Believe it!
3003-1

A.R.E. PRESS ● VIRGINIA BEACH ● VIRGINIA

ISBN 87604-062-8

Eleven printings of original text
Twelve printings of revised text

24th Printing, May 1997

Printed in the U.S.A.

TABLE OF CONTENTS

Foreword

"In the beginning God . . . " The first four words of the Bible strike deep and true into the human heart, for you and I are a part of that beginning. We are a part of God, created by Him when He created the heaven and the earth. His first command was, "Let there be light." And there was light.

This light, according to Edgar Cayce, was not the light of the sun. It was the light of the Son made manifest: the Christ, the only begotten of the Father. Hence His moving promise, "I am the light of the world: he that followeth me shall not walk in darkness, but shall have the light of life." (John 8:12)

Without light, this would be a derelict planet. Christ, then, is the pure essence of life eternal, and His light has guided the paths of the mystics since the beginning.

God spoke to Moses out of a burning bush.

The cloud which protected the Israelites from the burning sun in the daytime became a pillar of fire when it was necessary for them to travel by night.

Thunder and lightning preceded the voice of God when He called Moses to Mount Sinai.

Moses' face and clothing shone like the sun, after his forty days on Mount Sinai.

The Light of His Star proclaimed His advent into the earth, guiding the wise men to where He lay.

Jesus said. "I am the light of the world." Is it any wonder then that the light of the physical world, the sun which symbolizes Him, was darkened when He, the source of this light, hung suspended between heaven and earth?

"There was a man sent from God, whose name was John. The same came for a witness to bear witness of the Light, that all men through Him might believe. He was not that Light, but was sent to bear witness of that Light. That was the true Light which lighteth every man that cometh into the world. He was in the world, and the world was made by Him, and the world knew Him not." (John 1:6-10)

"And after six days Jesus taketh Peter, James and John his brother and bringeth them up into an high mountain apart, and was transfigured before them and His face did shine as the sun, and His raiment was white as the light. And behold, there appeared unto them Moses and Elias talking with Him . . . While He yet spake, behold, a bright cloud overshadowed them; and behold a voice out of the cloud, which said 'This is my beloved Son in whom I am well pleased; hear ye Him!' " (Matt. 17:1-6)

On the day of Pentecost cloven tongues of fire hovered over the heads of the disciples as they experienced the descent of the Holy Ghost. From that time on they began to preach inspirationally and to perform many more miracles.

The light experienced by Paul on the road to Damascus was so bright that it blinded him for three days, but it also purified him. The haloes of the saints, as depicted in paintings, are examples of the emanation of light in those whose "eye is single." It was the Light of the Christ that illuminated the mind of the Gautama Buddha.

The same light filled the room of Jacob Boehme, the German cobbler, whose writings are eagerly studied today. This light filled the cave of Mohammed as he sought God. The prison cell of Starr Daily, who was in solitary confinement, filled with that light, and it changed his entire life. Edgar Cayce knew he had to see a white light before it was safe for him to leave his physical body in order to read the Akashic records.

It is that same light which we seek in meditation.

If sin prevents communication with God, how do we go about reinstating ourselves so that we can again receive His reassurance? Meditation is the doorway and the key. While prayer is direct supplication to God, meditation is the attuning of ourselves mentally, physically and spiritually to the Spirit within and without so that God may speak to us! It is simply a process of stilling ourselves mentally and physically in order to listen, to become aware, to feel His presence and to receive His guidance and His strength. This power to listen is a part of the sixth sense of man. It goes far beyond the sense of normal hearing. It penetrates to an inner awareness, an inner sensitivity which transcends all the other senses. Meditation lifts our consciousness to this higher level.

We know from the history of religion that the great prophets, the reformers and founders of new faiths, the men and women who walked with God, had all practiced this art of silence, of meditation. Jesus retired from the crowds to seek these periods of aloneness with God. It is by this means that we are all renewed, through an overflowing of the Holy Spirit into our lives.

Not only does the Holy Spirit strengthen, guide and inspire us to greater service to the cause of God and man, but also it enables us to know ourselves.

As we learn to know ourselves we become strengthened in the knowledge that we are His. Peace becomes ours when we know that He is with us, ever watchful, forgiving and loving. We have faith that all is well, despite the turbulence around us. This peace of mind and soul is the direct result of our efforts to know Him and to do His will. "Thou wilt keep him in perfect peace whose mind is stayed on Thee." (Isaiah 26:3)

Immanuel Kant wrote that no two things were a greater source of wonder to man than the starry heavens above and the moral laws within, and that the power within that moves us to awe and wonder of the heavens above, is the same power which condemns us when we transgress the moral laws within us. The heavens remind us of the Universal God, and the voice of conscience of the "personal Father" of Jesus.

Conscience, the still small voice, is the voice of the Divine within us, guiding our feet back to the path. Meditation is the way to greater awareness of the Divine.

Chapter One

THE THREE NECESSITIES FOR MEDITATION

Mastering the technique of meditation is not easy. There are three keys necessary if the aspirant would achieve any degree of success. The three keys to this door of communication with God are sincerity, enthusiasm and perseverance.

1. SINCERITY

Ask yourself these questions:

Do I really know who and what God is? Do I know Him personally as a loving Father, or do I just know *about* Him? More important, does He know me? Are we on speaking terms, or do we just nod occasionally?

Am I sincere in wanting to know God's will for me?

Do I give credit and honor to Him for all that I have and am?

Am I a channel for His love, His mercy, His grace in the world?

Am I a peacemaker with all with whom I associate?

Do I forgive and forget hurts and disappointments?

Is there room for improvement in my life?

Do I need to change? Moreover, am I willing to change?

If we find ourselves answering in the negative to most of these questions, we may begin to realize how greatly we need Him. His promise has ever been that if we believe, live by His laws, He will aid us swiftly when we call, no matter where we may happen to be.

If we have gone against His Spirit and His laws, there has to be sincerity in our repentance. As we become aware of our errors, we balance them by heightening our standards of conduct until they reflect our search for God.

We also ask forgiveness for the sins of omission: that which we might have done but did not do; the times we might have helped but did not; the smile of forgiveness which could have ended an unpleasant situation, but which we withheld; the smile of encouragement to a timid child or a hesitant soul, the smile of welcome to a newcomer ill at ease. What is so important about a smile? It is God smiling through you! And as man is the only creation of God that can smile, for His sake, smile!

We may have lost countless opportunities for service, but in God's mercy and time they will present themselves again. Therefore, we should never waste precious time in self-condemnation for mistakes of the past. This, too easily, can be false pride instead of remorse.

Nor do we have to pretend to be without fault. God does not dwell on the past; only on the now. What are we doing *now* about His laws, about our associations with our fellow man? Our relationship with our fellow man is an exact reflection of our relationship with God. Every morning is a new beginning in our lives. We can change now, today, this very moment if we will but put ourselves in His hands. Sin alone separates the soul from God, and all sin is selfishness.

Having appraised ourselves honestly, we can then decide whether we are really sincere in wanting to know God and His ways. Only then are we ready to move forward; for it is God who awakens us, through love, before the Christ who guides us mentally can manifest Himself to us through the Holy Spirit that sustains and strengthens us.

2. ENTHUSIASM

Webster's dictionary, in discussing the derivation of the word *enthusiasm* traces its roots to a Greek word which meant "to be inspired, or possessed by a god." Enthusiasm is an inner fire, an inner light seeking its own source. In meditation, this inner fire stimulates every cell of the body and every reflex of the brain to listen. An enthusiast is one who is on fire with purpose, completely convinced of the rightness of his mission. His radiance is infectious, he stimulates others with his spirit, which springs from his own spiritual awakening. He speaks with authority. The Pharisees resented the authority with which Jesus spoke, for he always spoke from within, from the Father.

Enthusiasm, wisely directed, lends us wings, because it is born of the primeval yearning of the soul to return to its Creator. It is a longing dormant in the fiber of every cell of the body. Awakened, it cries out, "Here I am, Lord, use me, direct me!"

How do we evoke enthusiasm for our search for God? By first examining those people who, from the beginning of time, have found

Him. By studying the lives of the mystics, we can become a part of their lives, share in their ecstasies and in their very real and human fears and doubts. Because they lived in God's presence, so will we, if only for a moment. This can begin a change in us, a yearning to experience the upward sweep which took them to such great heights. The deeds of the saints can inspire us to greater spiritual activity.

The Bible tells of our experiences with Him. Studying it in conjunction with efforts at meditation and prayer awakens the necessary enthusiasm to begin.

3. PERSEVERANCE

Perseverance is perhaps the most difficult key. We need to keep on, day after day, in the effort to re-establish our communion.

When we first attempt to harness the thoughts, to control the body, to sit still, we realize just how much the body controls us, mind and spirit.

The suggestions made in the Edgar Cayce readings are very simple. An attempt must be made every day, at the same time whenever possible, in the same chair, in the same room. Why? To condition the body and the subconscious mind to the fact that we mean business. The higher self will be in control, the "I am that I am." Most important is our determination to keep this appointment with regularity, wherever we are. It may come as a rueful surprise to find that to really control the mind, to keep it from wandering, to keep it focused on even the simplest prayer or affirmation, is like trying to control a wild horse. Determined patience, constant practice, appealing to the inner self for help in stilling the body and mind, bring eventual success.

The time it takes will depend on our will to succeed as well as the effort expended; but we need to remember that even the effort is counted in our favor.

We thus determine in our hearts and minds that this appointment with our Maker is the most important event of the day. It is the one appointment that we never break. That time, the ten or fifteen minutes, should be taken from the apex of the twenty-four hours, not squeezed in when we have nothing else to do. In the beginning we find that the mind is ingenious in its alibis and excuses. A rug must be cleaned at that precise moment; a letter has to be written; the dog walked; a telephone call has suddenly become urgent; certain shopping cannot wait, and so on. Seemingly a hundred and one duties present themselves. This is the body and the mind letting it be known that they object strongly to being controlled.

3

Even after we have succeeded to some extent in mastering meditation, there will always be days when it is more difficult than usual.

This question was asked of Edgar Cayce, the answer to which will prove helpful at this point.

Q-15. Why is it at times my meditation seems unsatisfactory?

A-15. For ye are *still* in the flesh. *Why* did He say "Father, why hast thou forsaken me?" Even when the world was being overcome, the flesh continued to rebel; for "When I *would* do good, *evil* is present with me – but, though I take wings and fly to the utmost parts of the heavens, Thou art there; though I make my bed in hell, Thou art there." So, when doubt and fear come, close thine *senses* to the *material* things and *lose* thineself *in* Him. Not that ye shall not be joyous in the things that partake of the pleasures even of life; for so did He – but keep thine consciousness ever alert, ready and willing to be the channel that will make known His love, and *He* will speak with thee! 281-3

Chapter Two

PHYSICAL PREPARATION FOR MEDITATION

Now let us examine the conditions most conducive to meditation, making it quite clear that when these are not possible, we should not forego the meditation period.

A clean room and a clean body are naturally important. The posture of the body should be one of relaxation, enabling one to forget its presence as much as possible. However, this should not be so relaxed as to put one to sleep.

We may experiment with music, incense, chants or prayers to clear the mind and quiet the body, until the best way is found. It will differ with the individual. Comfort is essential, so that the senses can be stilled sufficiently for the powers of the soul to be concentrated in a supreme effort — communion with God.

To facilitate concentration, a balance of the physical forces is important. This applies first of all to diet. We should confine it whenever possible to fresh fruits and vegetables grown locally. This is a matter of vibration. Foods grown in the vicinity respond to the vibrations of the local atmosphere, as does the body. Hence the body can better assimilate such foods. The readings advise us to eat three vegetables grown above the ground to one grown below in order to bring about the required balance.

Heavy meats, such as beef, especially rare beef, should be eaten infrequently. Pork and pork products, except for a moderate amount of bacon, should be avoided. Vegetables should not be cooked in animal fats. Foods, in general, should be broiled, baked or roasted, rather than fried. Fish, fowl and lamb are recommended for the sedentary worker. It takes hard physical labor to burn up the elements contained in beef, pork, pastries and sweets. If the body does not burn them up, they become drosses and begin to burn up the body.

The less acid the system contains, the less will it be subject to

5

colds, for cold germs cannot get a foothold unless the body is over-acid. Food plays an essential part in maintaining this balance; but we must also recognize that mental attitudes of peace, optimism and patience do even more to keep the body in proper balance, thus creating a natural immunization to illness.

The readings suggest drinking six to eight glasses of water daily to keep the alimentary canal cleansed. Exercise and proper rest are of equal importance. Neglect of the body, in any form, is sin. We should strive to be balanced in all things in order to fulfill our roles as His representatives in the earth. This makes the study of nutrition valuable in the approach to meditation. Prayer before meals aids the body in improving assimilation.

MENTAL PREPARATION

The Bible tells us not to approach the altar of God if we have anything against our neighbor. If this is true regarding an altar in a church, how much more important is this admonition when we consider approaching the very spirit of God Himself.

Our first task then, is to search our hearts and minds, removing as far as possible all resentment, hate and negative feelings. If we are at odds with anyone, we should make an effort at reconciliation. We must be willing to pray for our enemies, and try to do good to those who would harm us, if we hope to enter into the Holy of Holies. To ask forgiveness for past wrongs supplies us with the courage to approach God.

If we have difficulty in praying for someone who we feel has wronged us, the Prayer of Loving Indifference may be helpful:

"Lord, he is Thine, even as I am Thine. Do that which will bring peace and harmony between us."

The reason that this prayer is so effective is that ordinarily when we pray for someone with whom we are in conflict, it is with the attitude that he alone needs reforming. Condemnation in any form has never brought healing. In the Prayer of Loving Indifference we acknowledge that all of us have sinned in the sight of God. Then we ask for help for all concerned. The prayer contains no condemnation, no recrimination, no self-pity, only a desire for proper relationships of love and helpfulness.

Vengeful attitudes strengthen the sense of separation from God. To be antagonistic is to repudiate God. To force someone to our will is to depart from His ways. To argue fiercely is unwise, for "when the minds of men clash, the Spirit of God leaves."

In our mental preparation, let the soft answer that turneth away wrath be our watchword. The angry voice not only disturbs others, but also takes its toll of the speaker's body, mind and spirit by lowering his vibrations. Sound (which is vibration) spans the distance between the finite and the infinite, and thus affects the soul itself. That is why words, whether sung or spoken, have the power to make us kneel in repentance, or lift our hearts to God in worship; or as of old, by yelling war chants, arouse a lust for revenge and slaughter. The vibration of a sound can shatter a glass or destroy a bridge. Let us be sure we only use the sounds which open the gates leading to the Holy of Holies.

Just as the walls of Jericho tumbled to the dust when the trumpets blew for the seventh time, so do the vibrations resulting from our words, thoughts and deeds strengthen or destroy the barriers between us and God.

SPIRITUAL PREPARATION

Once more we must thoroughly examine our ideals and purposes. Surely the spiritual ideal was best expressed by Jesus who became the Christ. He did not deal with personalities, but always with principles. He was all things to all people. He was human yet He expressed in thought, word and deed the fact that He was the Son of the Living God. Through His activities and words, He proclaimed the fact that He walked and talked with His Creator. Through the love He gave so abundantly to all, He expressed the Father. He had control over Himself, and thus controlled all the elements. The flesh was subservient to His will; thus all of materiality was subject to His will, for He was one with God. Because of this, all power in heaven and on earth was given to Him.

A spiritual ideal, then, is to desire His will to be our will; His Way our way; and His Spirit our spirit.

Ideals are set from spiritual purposes, spiritual aspirations, spiritual desires and there is a pattern in Him who is the way, the truth and the light, and when that pattern is set according to such judgments, we would find there is never condemning of another. Because others do not agree with thee, condemn them not. For with what judgment ye mete, it is measured to thee again. These ye find as thy greater problems in the present in relationships with others. Then analyze first thyself and thy ideals. 5255-1

For those activities of man or woman in the earth may not excel . . . the individual's ideal. 3407-1

Only by holding fast to these mental, physical and spiritual ideals can we break through the confines of the ego. Only then can we hope to behold the fulfillment of the Biblical promise: "I will not

7

leave you comfortless, I will come to you." (John 14:18)

When that hour comes, the awareness given us at our creation will again restore the soul to the purpose for which it was created — companionship with God.

Once we understand our motives clearly, we are ready to pursue the art of meditation. For most people, the use of an affirmation hastens attunement to the spiritual. Here are four key examples taken from *A Search for God,* Volume I.

Father, as we seek to see and know Thy face, may we each, as individuals and as a group, come to know ourselves even as we are known, that we — as lights in Thee — may give the better concept of Thy spirit in this world.   262-5

God, be merciful to me. Help Thou my unbelief. Let me see in Him that Thou would have me see in my fellow man. Let me see in my brother that which I see in Him that I worship.   262-11

Let virtue and understanding be in me, for my defense is in Thee, O Lord, my redeemer; for Thou hearest the prayer of the upright in heart.   262-17

Create in me a pure heart, O God. Open Thou my heart to the faith Thou hast implanted in all that seek Thy face. Help Thou mine unbelief in my God, in my neighbor, in myself.   262-13

A WAITING PERIOD

These affirmations serve the purpose of stilling the mind and awakening the divine activities within. The prayer is directed to the higher self, which then subdues the ego and permits the unencumbered soul to respond.

For most of us there will follow a waiting period. The movement and expansion of the soul to a higher vibration of awareness is taking place at the unconscious level. The only reason that we are not consciously aware of this is because our line of communication is not yet clear enough. God has not turned away. He is ever ready to guide, strengthen and help; for His promise has ever been "they may walk in my statutes, and keep mine ordinance, and do them; and they shall be my people, and I will be their God." (Ezekiel 11:20)

This waiting period can be difficult, but from the Bible we have the reassurance that our patience will be rewarded: "Wait on the Lord, be of good courage, and He shall strengthen thine heart. Wait, I say, on the Lord." (Psalm 27:14)

This period of hiatus, this patient waiting for a response is much like being alone in the house at night, straining your ears for an unfamiliar sound. Suddenly, you begin to listen intently, not only with your mind but with your whole being, with every cell of your

8

body. Regarding this intensification of consciousness, Alexis Carrel, in *Man the Unknown*, writes that the soul of man is not in his brain, as was the classical assumption. Man's entire body, he states, is actually a projection of consciousness, "a substratum of mental and spiritual energies."

Alert receptivity, then, is essential. When the mind wanders, we must coax it gently back to the prayer. Often, simply calling God by name will bring stillness. This is a rewarding means of reaching a state of mental repose.

However, in using any affirmation, it is helpful to analyze the meaning of each phrase prior to the meditation period, so that the attention may be clearly focused on the essence. The mind should not wander in search of other possible meanings during meditation. The total essence of the ideal expressed becomes the focus of attention, thus bringing attunement with the deeper spiritual aspirations.

Focus on the affirmation, is however, just the beginning of meditation. There are usually three stages — concentration, quiet expectancy and finally union with the Most High.

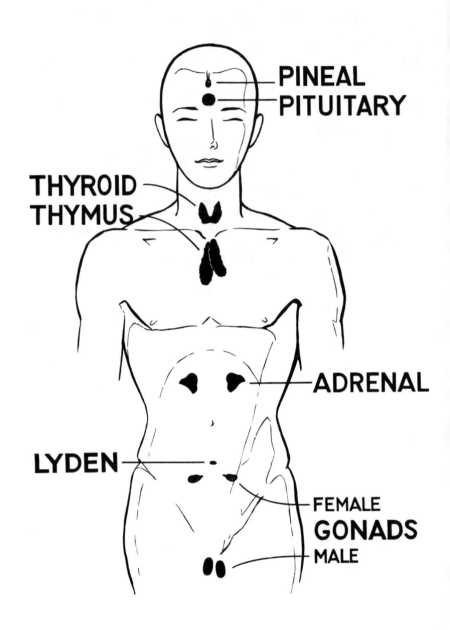

PINEAL
PITUITARY

THYROID
THYMUS

ADRENAL

LYDEN

FEMALE
GONADS
MALE

Chapter Three

THE SPIRITUAL CENTERS

The purification of the spiritual body takes place within the endocrine glands, under the direction of the mind. Endocrinology and knowledge of the proper functioning of these glands and their hormones is still in its infancy. Dr. John A. Schindler, in his book, *How to Live 365 Days a Year,* states that the body knows the secret of optimal hormone balance, even if we do not. He maintains that we can encourage optimal hormone balance by providing our bodies with the stimulus of pleasant and cheering emotions. Constructive emotions, he said, are just as beneficial to the glands as destructive emotions are harmful.

The Edgar Cayce readings concur with this principle that constructive thoughts and emotions release healing hormones into the body and mind.

"Don't forget," Dr. Schindler adds, "that constructive emotions have two general effects. First, they replace the negative emotions which were producing stress effects; and secondly, they create their own pituitary condition, which is an optimal balance of endocrine function."

The readings go further. They suggest that the endocrine glands are the spiritual centers of the body and that through them our spiritual forces, which are the vital forces of the body, find means of expression.

These centers are the gonads, the lyden (cells of Leydig), the adrenals, the thymus, the thyroid and parathyroids, the pineal and the pituitary glands. The proper application of the energies illuminates them, transforming the individual into a light in the world.

Ideals enter the mind when led by the spirit. The readings remind us over and over again that mind is the builder, led by the spirit we are entertaining, the spirit of God or the spirit of the devil — self. What one thinks and eats, one becomes.

11

Spiritual cleansing begins when the mind is in accord with His spirit. It is across the bridge of the mind that we pass, as we come to know God. Once a soul sets for itself an ideal which is spiritual in essence, every cell in the body is made aware of this and changes begin to take place. Our seven spiritual centers become the points of contact with the Divine within; thus we experience a stepping-up of activity in all these centers. We have redirected the use of this energy to its highest function. A refining process has taken place in the body, a lifting of the rate of vibration; these centers now disseminate their energies and hormones to the entire body. This raising of the rate of vibration is essential; it insures the body against any harmful effects from the intensity of the power it is now capable of receiving. The protection, then, exists not only in the ideal that is held, but also in the follow-through, the putting of it into practice.

Chemical changes result from constructive attitudes; an increase in the secretion of hormones in the blood stream brings greater balance to the body, the mind and the emotions.

As the individual sits in meditation, his mind focused on an affirmation, spiritual energy begins to move upward from the gonads. Usually, at this point, a pulsation may be felt at the end of the spine. A vibration akin to electricity, beginning with the toes and rising to the top of the head, may also manifest itself. Sometimes this electrical vibration comes in billowing waves, running the entire course of the body and ending in a "fullness" of the hands or the head. Circulation and nerve energy are involved. These are but physical manifestations of the spiritual energy which is coming into being.

Sometimes one may experience the sensation of a short-circuit in the body, should impurities be present in an area near one of the glands. The newly released spiritual energy is knocking at the "gates" or "doors" of these spiritual centers.

"Lift up your heads, O ye gates; and be lifted up, ye everlasting doors; and the King of Glory shall come in. Who is this King of Glory? The Lord strong and mighty, the Lord mighty in battle." (Psalm 24: 7-8)

This short-circuiting may occur in any area. Just as crackling noises and sparks emanate from shorted electrical equipment in the home, so can the body react in the experimental stages of an attempt to establish contact with the Source of all Power.

The human cause may stem from a poor physical condition, from hate, prejudice, willfulness, or some other negative emotion. Adhesions from accidents or operations can also account for undue pressures on these centers whose function it is to open the doors to other dimensions of experience. Meditation, however, will open all these doors with safety. For example, if the spiritual force has been able to rise unhindered and undefiled to the pineal and pituitary, one may experience an incandescence as if the whole body had been filled with light and become transparent.

It is at the pineal center that we gradually become oriented to the Christ-presence, where we may even receive the mind of Christ, depending on the degree of the attunement.

This force then flows into the pituitary, from whence, being now in purified form, it flows downward, cleansing and strengthening body and mind. It is necessary to keep this spiritualized tide in motion every day, in order that growth may be constant. With this increasing purpose, the soul ultimately becomes a channel for His fulfillment in the earth.

Just as the physical body loses strength and becomes faint if it does not receive its daily food, so does the spiritual body weaken if it does not receive its daily bread. The forces elevated in meditation are the "daily bread" referred to in the Lord's Prayer. This is the same "bread of life" spoken of by the Master Jesus, when He said, "I am the bread of life." (John 6:35)

And Jesus also said, "He that believeth on me, as the Scripture hath said, out of his belly shall flow rivers of living water." (John 7:38) The movement of these spiritual forces in meditation are the "rivers of living water."

There are many other physical manifestations that may occur during the period of meditation, all related to the movement of this spiritual force. There are the electrical impulses which seem at times to sway the body from side to side, or backward and forward or in a circular motion. This is usually a phenomenon of inner movement only, but it is possible for it to extend into actual movement of the body. All three movements are expressions of the three-dimensional world, the material plane.

A sensation of warmth, a dancing sensation in the eyes suggests healing power. A heaviness of the wrists and a vortex of power at the palms of the hands are further signs of this power.

What is healing power but God-power or energies released for the purpose of serving God and man? What releases the power? The purpose, the prayer, and then the waiting on God.

The more we become able to still the conscious mind, the more trouble we can expect from the subconscious mind, for it is the conscious mind of the soul. It, too, must be purified. We have stimulated this area of the mind as a result of the ideal we have up-held; attitudes and thoughts previously concealed in the subconscious rise to the surface for examination. Symbols and old familiar scenes begin to flash before us like pictures on a screen. However, this is still only the beginning of meditation. We should not dwell too long on these pictures but press on to the silence. In other words, we must return attention to the affirmation.

We may at this point be fascinated by the many faces appearing, or numerous pairs of eyes staring. We may even hear our names called; we may feel as if we were in the midst of a crowd, listening to chatter and laughter. We must not stop there, for we are not yet in real meditation. Of course, it is fascinating at first, for it is an entirely new experience. The sounds, the voices, the pictures, the eyes and faces may all belong to souls already in the beyond who, having seen the light pouring through the open door (the spiritual center), have been attracted. It is much akin to the sensation of looking through a strange keyhole, only to see another eye looking back. Intriguing, perhaps, but neither stands to gain much from such a restricted encounter.

We must leave this entertainment behind and "press on to the mark of the high calling," His mark, the superconscious, the Christ Consciousness, the "hill of the Lord."

It should be stated here that for some people nothing apparently occurs; however, "that which is needful" is being given. In a definitive answer to someone who had asked for the essential steps in meditation, Edgar Cayce said, "Keep faithful. Keep alive. Keep true. Keep impersonal. Keep going on!" (281-9) This is imperative for anyone who wants to meditate.

Jesus reminded us that only the heathen seek constantly for signs and wonders; so let us persist, despite the fact that no rewards are ostensibly forthcoming at the moment we want them.

The readings tell us that when we open ourselves in meditation, we "loosen" our conscious mind to all levels of consciousness, to all time and space, and thus to all the soul's experiences from the beginning of time. Because we have existed from the beginning, we are, under exceptional conditions, able to read the akashic records and tap the collective unconscious of man. We must be very careful to enter worthily into meditation, lest we stray unawares to a level that could be hostile to us. There are as many unfriendly "places" over on that other side of life as there are here on our own plane of consciousness.

The earth is a proving ground where we must learn to love one another. It is also a testing place for the soul, the preparatory school for the real spiritual life which is to follow. As Jesus said, "A new commandment I give unto you, That ye love one another as I have loved you . . . By this shall all men know that ye are my disciples, if ye have love one to another." (John 13:34, 35)

This spiritual height is reached by attunement to the Creative Forces in meditation. The release of energy should never be forced by such methods as exercise, or holding the breath, or by focusing one's mind on a special center, or by willing the centers to open. When meditation is properly approached, these centers will open voluntarily. The knowledge, power and illumination of the soul which accompany this opening will then be concentrated on the good of others and not to one's own misdoing.

The opening of the centers should come only as a result of spiritual growth, not through any abnormal means. Unless the power released is used to express His spirit with and for others, it will but inflame our lower natures.

THE GONADS

The glands of reproduction are the reservoirs of the life force. They house the creative energy of the body. As the individual sits in silence, having lifted his mind by use of the Lord's Prayer (an excellent affirmation), creative energy is released at this level. This energy now carries the stamp of the Divine, because both the purpose and the thought which released it were holy.

The lyden gland (cells of Leydig), control-center of the soul's activity, opens its doors to this energy, enabling the mind of the soul — the subconscious — to rise to the pineal, seat of the Christ Consciousness. This energy is then transmitted to the other centers of the body by means of the pituitary. As it passes through the centers, it illuminates them.

This process has an impressive parallel. The readings indicate that the creation of this new "spiritual man within" follows the same pattern of evolution as the foetus in the womb of the mother. At conception the spermatozoa and the ovum combine to create the nature of the body-to-be. As the division of the cells begins, the first gland to be formed is the pituitary. The creative forces then move from the pituitary to the adrenals and then to the other five glands of the body. As in meditation the glands are illuminated by this creative energy, so also in the creation of the physical body the glands are illuminated into their own activity of growth. The processes are identical.

Just as the ideal behind the Creative Force in meditation serves as the apotheosis of the new character, so, when the force is used solely for selfish purposes, it creates a Frankenstein monster.

It is always the purpose which determines whether an activity is selfish or unselfish. The energy of the gonads, used wholly on the sexual level and without control, may bring sexual perversions and unbridled sensuality. In Biblical terminology, do we bear the mark of the Lamb or the mark of the beast?

Purpose is the deciding factor in the nature of the new body created in the womb of the mother. This purpose in the minds of the parents at the time of conception determines aspects of the consciousness of the unborn child. Harmonious preparation for parenthood, then, is vitally important. This first impulse behind the act of creation, either in meditation or in intercourse, takes permanent precedent in the pituitary gland, which is the master-gland of the body.

The spiritual power generated by meditation can be harnessed in the service of inspirational writing or speaking. The ability to compose beautiful music or to create great works of art springs from the same source. The soul is enabled to express itself creatively in whatever medium attracts it most.

In Alexis Carrel's *Man the Unknown,* the author states that the genital glands influence the strength and quality of the mind, and that in this regard no other gland can be compared in importance.

He makes the point that the greatest contributors to literature and the arts are persons who are strongly sexed. He feels that this also holds true for the great saints and for world conquerors. He finds that there is an alteration of the mental state of an individual when the genital glands are removed. In both men and women the change can be a vital one, affecting intellectual activity, moral sense or personality.

Possibly this truth has been known for centuries on either a conscious or unconscious level, for the theme appears in both literature and music. The mutilation of Abelard may well have been assumed to have been the cause of his cowardice which stands in such dramatic contrast to the passion and sacrifice of Heloise.

The belief has been held that unrequited love often fills a creative purpose when it stimulates the mind and the imagination. Artistic inspiration, as well as religious inspiration, seems to correlate in some way with the condition of the sex glands. However, if as Dr. Carrel concludes, the great artists were great lovers, he also reminds us that sexual excesses impede intellectual activity. Therefore although intelligence is dependent on well-developed sex glands, it is also dependent on the discipline of those glands. Repression of sexual

16

appetites has the tendency to cause the unbalanced person to become more abnormal, yet such repression seems to add strength to those already strong. In this way, we are led to see that not only are sex glands of primary importance, but so are our attitudes toward them and our control of the appetites arising from them. Once again we see the individual's opportunity for the exercise of his free will.

The gonads are referred to in the readings as the motor of the body. They supply the power to lift the forces of creative energy to and through all the spiritual centers during meditation. Meditation, then, is the means whereby this life force is given a new purpose, a new idea, a new use.

Mind, directed by the spirit, enforced by the will, begins to build the new person, the New Jerusalem, the new heaven and earth spoken of in The Revelation (21:1). All these terms refer to the newly awakened soul.

"And I will give them one heart, and I will put a new spirit within you; and I will take the stony heart out of their flesh, and will give them an heart of flesh; that they may walk in my statutes, and keep mine ordinances, and do them; and they shall be my people, and I will be their God." (Ezekiel 11: 19, 20)

The individual, then, has a choice as to what he will do with this God-given force. However, it must be used and we must choose. Joshua said: "As for me and my house, we will serve the Lord." (Joshua 24:15) How do we serve the Lord through the forces of the gonads? By spiritualizing physical desires through meditation, which gives us the insight and the necessary strength to fulfill our purpose in the earth; to be about our Father's business.

Chapter Four

THE LYDEN GLANDS (Cells of Leydig)

Lyden means sealed. This gland, located in and above the gonads, is the starting point of the soul's activity. It is the door through which the soul may go on to higher realms of consciousness. When the soul has lost touch with God, this center of fertility becomes sterile. The soul out of touch with its Maker becomes confused. The seeds of self-doubt spring up like weeds. An intense feeling of being alone and persecuted is the usual fate of such a soul. Overwhelming bouts of depression may descend on him, violent enough to take the form of schizophrenia.

In America today, this is the fastest growing mental illness. We do not have enough doctors to give adequate care to these cases. In experiments performed by biologists, the plasma from the blood stream of a schizophrenic was fed to flies, which in turn were eaten by spiders. These spiders began to spin loose, shapeless webs. The blood plasma from other mental diseases had little or no effect on them, but the schizophrenic's plasma was proved to contain a substance which has been temporarily and forebodingly identified as "X." In the biologists' opinion, it is an unique substance manufactured by the patient's own body.

Some attribute it to the malfunctioning of an endocrine gland. But what imbalance causes the malfunctioning? Is it physical or emotional?

As yet, there is no medical answer; but according to the readings of Edgar Cayce, this deterioration is a result of a malfunctioning of the soul, expressing itself through the endocrine glands. This is directly related to its purpose in the earth. Mind is the builder, guided by the spirit. What is spirit? The force which directs our life. Some doctors have stated that all schizophrenics are preoccupied solely with themselves. Could this illness possibly have its origin in a morbid self-preoccupation? If it can, then self-preoccupation is powerful enough to separate a soul from God.

18

To be separated from God is also to lose touch with one's fellow man, which means the loss of that rapport with others which is essential to a sense of balanced well-being. This separation chokes and destroys the life force which supplies all peace and harmony within.

This emphasizes even more urgently the importance of meditation and prayer, which govern the transformation so necessary to us. For all of us suffer from some form of selfishness, and which of us is not slightly psychotic at times? The forces released in meditation open spiritual centers which give us insight into our true natures. This stimulates better and clearer thinking. These constructive thoughts then stimulate the glands to release healing hormones in proportion to the body's needs. Thus does the healing take place in the spirit, the body and the mind. We refer here to the mind of the soul; not the brain through which the conscious mind operates in the physical body.

All healing is of God, and comes from within. Whether it be a prayer, a poultice, medication or surgery; all are for the purpose of creating a harmonious balance within the body so that the forces of God within may heal. For who planted the herbs or plants that bring healing? Who gave wisdom to the mind of man? Who gave skill to the surgeon's hand? Who created the mind of man in His image so that healing would be possible?

When meditation is used as the healing agent, the beneficent effects may come slowly, husbanded by the increased sensitivity of mind and spirit; but meanwhile it strengthens the individual by distributing a proper balance of hormonal activity throughout the endocrine system.

Stimulated by this spiritualization, the lyden assumes its rightful place and influence, bringing to the individual the best qualities of the male and female. The man will develop the virtues of gentleness, patience, love, tenderness, graciousness, generosity and moral strength. The woman will develop the virtues of courage, practicality, order, logic, resoluteness and greater intellectual abilities.

The balancing of attributes was evidenced in the life of Jesus. In his book, *Growing Spiritually,* E. Stanley Jones examines these balancing facets in the life of the Master. Dr. Jones writes that Jesus was both militant and passive. The militant or active side, he says, is shown in the fact that He was projecting the most redemptive movement, the Kingdom of God, into the whole of life, to change life. The fact that He put up no resistance on His way to the cross, exemplifies His passivity. That Jesus was at once both terrible and tender — tender at the graveside of a friend, terrible in His wrath when driving the moneychangers from the temple. "Behold the man," Pilate was to say, yet Dr. Jones points out that even while He manifested the strength of the man, He manifested also the softness of the woman. In this perfect balance of characteristics we see the illustrations of the duality of Creative Forces.

The sublimation of purely physical desires must eventually be achieved by all of us if we are to become channels for the Christ Spirit.

THE ADRENAL GLANDS

The adrenal glands are located on the upper anterior surface of the kidneys. Shaped like a cocked hat, they illustrate how extensively man has developed his emotions, in that they are larger in man than in any other animal.

We are actively aware of this center in times of stress, when it pours adrenalin into the blood stream to aid us in fighting, fleeing, defending ourselves or performing some unusual feat of physical prowess. The adrenals are also the storehouse of our emotional karma, accumulated in other life experiences. Here, too, we store our anxieties. From this center comes the energy negatively expended in gossip, anger, hate, argument and grudges.

The constant negative use of energy at this level induces emotional instability, high blood-pressure, and certain types of heart disease. Cancer often has its roots in deep-seated hatreds or resentments, whether from this life or another. Prejudice is another form of hate too willingly indulged by far too many people. Even the ulcer, status symbol of the executive, results from repressed tensions and anxieties.

The effect of thought on man's physical body was also discussed by Dr. Carrel in *Man the Unknown.* He concluded that each state of consciousness probably has a corresponding expression organically. He suggests that when various negative emotions or attitudes become habitual, they might very well be responsible for various physical changes and definite diseases. Much has been published in recent years to substantiate the theory that worry, strain, and tension are directly responsible for the early deaths among business men. The importance of the emotions to the glands, and in turn, their importance to the health of the body make it essential that we pay attention to both our thoughts and our emotions.

When, in meditation, the life force passes through the adrenals, a change for the better begins at once. Slowly but surely this energy, guided by the spiritual ideals in the mind, brings persistence, courage, drive, patience and the ability to be quiet and silent. The negative emotions have no room to move; they are literally squeezed out, for the same energy, once used negatively is now being used constructively.

As we all know, the chronic worrier lives in a state of permanent exhaustion. All negative emotions burn up energy. They also prevent the body from renewing and rebuilding itself. To hold animosities of any kind is to seal up the drosses and poisons in the body. Once we master the art of changing our attitudes, miraculous changes begin to take place in us. As the adrenal center becomes purified through the proper application of positive energy, mediumship may be developed. There is a theory that psychometry works through this center also.

Application of the fruits of the Spirit enable the individual to make constructive use of his emotions in seeing and seeking out the good and the beautiful. He then becomes a greater channel for the good, or God, in life.

THE THYMUS GLAND

The thymus gland, the least known, is found behind the heart in the upper thoracic area. It is larger in children than in adults, and larger in women than in men. The latest discoveries seem to indicate that it contains the master plan for the white blood cells. In the embryo, it is the thymus that first manufactures these cells. The white blood cells are the scavengers, the guardians of the body.

In an article entitled "Thymus Back in Favor," by Dr. T.R. Van-Dellen (*The Houston Post,* February 1963), we read that "experimental studies by Dr. Robert A. Goode of the University of Minnesota indicate a possible link between the malfunctioning of the thymus gland and a number of baffling diseases. In addition, two active hormones have been isolated from the gland.

"A few decades or more ago, the thymus was in disgrace. It was blamed for pressure on the windpipe in infants, and X-ray treatments were employed to decrease the size of the gland. Now we know this therapy had little value.

"The thymus, as of 1963, has gained considerably in repute. It is extremely active in early life as the source of lymphoid tissues that are responsible for immunity from disease. These cells are capable of migrating from the gland, to reproduce in other parts of the body.

"Disease enters the picture when the thymus becomes lazy. As a result, the body's defenses are lowered and the outcome may be rheumatoid arthritis, leukemia, and other unusual blood disorders. Malfunctioning of this gland may also occur when a tumor develops on the thymus.

"Research on laboratory animals showed that removal of the structure early in life produces an immunologically crippled rabbit or mouse. These animals were unable to produce anti-bodies, the body's first line of defense against disease. This does not occur when the thymus is removed at maturity, lending weight to the theory that the immunity pattern is established early in life."

Since the thymus is related to the heart it is associated with love. The Bible substantiates the view of the readings regarding the heart: "For man looketh on the outward appearance, but the Lord looketh on the heart." (I Sam. 16:7) "Search me, O God, and know my heart." (Psalm 139:23) "The heart is deceitful above all things." (Jer. 17:9) On the surface the intent may seem benign, but if the motive is selfish, the heart is most certainly deceitful.

It seems fair to assume that one of man's innate protectors against disease lies in the proper functioning of the thymus. Could we keep it active, rather than allowing it to harden as it does early in life, we might discover this to be the center from which comes extra protection. Since the purpose of our experiences in the earth is to learn to love one another, if we fail in this purpose we fail to safeguard the gland which immunizes us against disease and illness.

Since the thymus is associated with love and purpose, let us examine love itself. Love is scarcely recognized by most of us, let alone practiced. Love in essence is giving, giving, giving, without thought of reciprocation or even appreciation. Too often we love others for our own sake rather than for theirs. We love them because they give us joy, not because we give them joy by serving them. Mother-love is perhaps the highest example we have in the earth of genuinely unselfish love. Not "smother love," but the "God love" that gives and gives and gives with wise purpose, subordinating self.

In the Cayce readings the following ideas are expressed: First, love is that expressed in a baby's smile; the hope, the light, the seeking and the expression of that which (in a baby) is love undefiled. The next may be seen in the rose as it seeks, with that which it has, to express that beauty which will glorify its Maker. The next may be found in friendship; the kind which is without thought of self, which brings the expression of love glorified through the attunement that comes with friendship. The next we find manifested in the reasons for the beauty of a song; the harmony that is the expression of the soul within, whether in instruments or in the voice raised in praise to the Giver of Light. The next expression is in duty fulfilled without thought of self, in a loving way. The next is in speech, by giving encouragement, speaking a kind word, being gentle in speech. The next is in the glory expressed through a contented heart that knows it has taken advantage of every opportunity to serve, by going out of the way to make the lot of a neighbor more joyous and brighter. Love is expressed in the looking forward to those days when greater and greater may be the opportunities to serve Him. This is also expressed when your own little child grasps your hand. This is not of the emotions alone, but the love of God for man.

The purest example of perfect love, of course, is the love of Jesus. On the cross, despite His agony of body and mind, His thoughts were all for others. Even his tormentors came under His protection in the words "Father, forgive them, for they know not what they do." (Luke 23:24)

There was the love of Ananias for Paul, who had come to Damascus to imprison him. Yet after the conversion on the road to Damascus had left Paul blind and helpless, Ananias, being instructed in a vision, went to Paul and greeted him as a brother, then placed his hands on him and restored his sight.

There was the love of David for his son Absalom, who desired to wrest the kingdom from his father, by patricide if necessary. Yet David instructed that not a hair of his head should be touched. When Absalom was killed, David's heart-rending cry was: "Oh my son Absalom, my son, my son Absalom! Would God I had died for thee, O Absalom, my son, my son!" (II Sam. 18:33)

There was the love of Lincoln as he openly wept for the slain of both armies.

The readings suggest that pure love is non-sexual love. Giving, with no thought of receiving. The antithesis of love thrives in the egotism bred by envy, jealousy, lust, possessiveness, greed, arrogance, self-pity and self-abasement. When we become impatient and intolerant, self-righteousness has stepped between us and love. Love implies patience with self and with others. This is the birth of divine love. To love others is to love God and self. To be content with others is a sign of contentment with self. To be content is to be in rapport with God, acting with His spirit. This rapport with Him results in a rapport with all of His creations — man, animal and nature. Love opens the door to true understanding and empathy with one's fellows.

When George Washington Carver was asked what system he used to develop the peanut he answered, "I didn't have to *do* anything! I just loved them!"

Love opens all doors. Another word for love is, of course, understanding. Love and understanding are interdependent. At this center, then, love is awakened, bringing with it consideration, unselfishness, sincerity and honesty.

Chapter Five

THE THYROID GLAND

The thyroid, located in the throat, is related to will-power. The thyroid is somewhat like a horseshoe in shape. A horseshoe has long been accepted as a sign of good luck. If one's will is God's will, then one enjoys good fortune in life; it is God's expression of appreciation to the soul.

From the misuse of the will for selfish and domineering ends, may come the condition known as hyper-thyroidism. When little effort is made to use the will at all, the opposite may be encountered, an imbalance known as hypo-thyroidism. In the first, an excess of thyroxin is produced, causing nervousness and excitability, while in the second, apathy saps the vitality. Again, we see the importance of balance and moderation in the choices we make.

Therefore, let us always pray, "Not my will, O Lord, but Thine."

The idea that man misapplies his will was examined at length by Bishop Fulton J. Sheen. He wrote that virtue, to the pagan Aristotle, was actually the middle path between two extremes. He was careful to point out that if, for example, the opposite of drunkenness was simply a hearty condemnation of the evils of alcohol, then it wouldn't be a virtue. The whole challenge of life is to choose a path that avoids all extremes.

The Bishop pointed out that virtue is very much like a footpath with ditches on either side, into which it is most easy to fall should one lose his footing. The pathway of moderation, then, is not an easy one to follow, for the danger of going from one extreme to the other is always present. He used the example of the ditches to symbolize illusions that beset men on their way through life: the illusion that one has no need of salvation, he said, is the "ditch of presumption," and its extreme, the illusion that one is so bad that he is beyond salvation, is the "ditch of despair."

The only hope for man, therefore, is the pathway between

24

the two, the pathway of faith.

Continuing his metaphorical explanation, he also compared moderation to a highway with an abyss on each side, one of wasteful extravagance, and one of miserliness. He explained that the proper function of moderation is to govern tendencies and desires within us, which, although in no way evil in themselves, could become evil if allowed to become the ruling forces in an individual.

In addition to looking at the desires of the body which we know as physical appetites, he looked also at desires of the mind, such as the desire for knowledge. While this is in itself a laudable desire, when a man carries it to the extreme of thinking that he knows everything, he becomes unteachable.

Any desire that a man allows to become an obsession becomes dangerous to him. When his desire to own property becomes a desire to own more property than anyone else, or when he desires power for its own sake, he should remember the admonition of the Master: "For what shall it profit a man, if he shall gain the whole world, and lose his own soul?" (Mark 8:36)

Bishop Sheen admitted that it might be argued that moderating one's drives and instincts would be, in effect, a stifling of self-expression. However, he states that although our wants should be satisfied according to nature, that nature is rational. Our self-indulgence of either our likes or our dislikes must be controlled by moderation.

The philosophy that came through the late Edgar Cayce is wholly in accord with this prominent churchman's thesis. The readings were careful to emphasize, as did he, that one extreme can be as bad as the other. The swing must never be from one pole to another, but rather to the middle pathway between them. It is a lesson most sorely needed in our land at this time, for here, through the various media of mass communication, new and artificial desires are being created all the time, and an inflated economy tends to push aside or ignore the old-fashioned virtue of moderation. Restraint and control of any kind have become in many ways alien ideas. We need to remember that there is a great difference between desire and need. There is no limit to the list of our wants, but our actual needs have definite limits. We should examine and evaluate our wants with a willingness to admit how many of them have been imposed on our consciousnesses from outside ourselves. We must realize that the fulfillment of all our material wishes is less than a guarantee of happiness; such fulfillment might only intensify unhappiness. Self-restraint is necessary for soul growth; in fact, Bishop Sheen says that

25

the restraint which we apply reveals the condition of our spiritual health just as our pulse reveals the condition of our physical health.

Meditation becomes the controlling factor in making the right choices. When the energies flowing through the thyroid center are in accord with His will, clairvoyance, clairaudience, telepathy and the psychic sense of smell and taste may be developed. Not all people develop the same gifts, obviously; but whichever gift best serves the individual will be his or hers to develop.

It is worthy of note that in some cases where there has been a growth on the thyroid, a degree of clairvoyance, clairaudience or telepathy has developed. When surgery removed the growth, the sensitivity disappeared also. This indicates that the sensitivity was originally caused by the unnatural pressure or constriction on the thyroid.

In meditation, the energy released upon the thyroid brings about this same sensitivity by opening a door into the psychic realms of consciousness.

The more materialistic we are, the denser we are spiritually. Through prayer, meditation, right thinking and right eating, the body, the mind and the spirit become lighter and more receptive to the spiritual atmosphere. We begin to perceive new and distant horizons. The fog of materialism has lifted, and ESP is free to manifest itself. According to the readings, the thyroid is one of the three most spiritual centers — the gateway to the highest centers in the body.

THE PINEAL GLAND

This gland situated a little above the pituitary is the "Mind of Christ" center. When this center has been truly awakened, one may experience holy communion.

This center, when stimulated daily, brings seership or prophecy. Through this center comes the ability to remember past experiences in the earth. From this center comes the light that goes to the pituitary and spills over, cleansing and purifying the body, mind and soul. This is also the symbolic "fountain of youth" which Ponce de Leon sought.

If this center is kept active through meditation, the body will keep itself rejuvenated for as long as it is beneficial to the soul. Moses, after forty rugged years circling the desert, was still youthful. "And Moses was an hundred and twenty years old when he died; his eye was not dim, nor his natural force abated." (Deut. 34:7)

It is at this center that the mind of the soul meets the Holy Spirit, the Paraclete, the Comforter. This was the experience of the disciples on the day of Pentecost. Following the descent of the Holy

26

Ghost, they all began to prophesy and heal.

The descent of the Holy Ghost enabled the disciples to overcome fear and to speak in tongues that all could understand. It enabled them to endure every extreme of suffering and persecution. It endowed them with visions and dreams of a precognitive and retrocognitive nature; it brought them guidance, direction and encouragement. When their wills were aligned with God's will, through the pineal came the Spirit of Christ, cleansing and raising the vibrations of all the lower centers.

Holy Communion as practiced in the churches is the formalized ritual of this inward communion, which is possible to every child of God.

The creative holy force rising to the pineal center is the bread from within, or His body; the Holy Ghost descending is His Holy Spirit, His blood, or the Spirit of His blood. These are blended at the area of the pineal. To partake of His body and His blood is to be sustained by the holy forces within, which have been purified by Him. It is through trying to live His purposes, to walk in His footsteps, to shed the blood of all selfish physical desires, that we experience true communion through the descent of the Holy Ghost.

After Jesus' baptism in the river Jordan, it was the descent of the Holy Ghost in the form of a dove which brought Him the necessary fortitude to undergo the crucifixion, thus proving forever the dominion of love over hell, death, and the grave.

The Holy Ghost is the Holy Comforter promised by Jesus when He said in John (15:26, 27), "But when the Comforter is come, whom I will send unto you from the Father, even the Spirit of Truth which proceedeth from the Father, he shall testify of me; and ye also shall bear witness because ye have been with me from the beginning."

With the mind of Christ comes wisdom, for the individual can then measure that which bears the mark of God, or good, by the degree to which it lifts his soul to a greater awareness of God. Only through the Son, represented by the pineal, can we come to the Father, represented by the pituitary.

THE PITUITARY GLAND

This gland is the master-gland of the body. It is situated between the eyes at the center of the brain. The pituitary is referred to in the readings as the seat of contact with the Father, the superconscious, which is not of the earthly forces at all. It is through the pituitary, the highest spiritual center, that ultimate awakening comes.

In the mental it is that which gives judgment and understanding, tolerance AND relationships to the determining factors. Hence we find some grow old

27

gracefully, some tolerantly, some fussily and some very meanly. All of these, then, are the expressions of that which has been the dominant force that began from its first active influence that passed from its innate to the animate, to its full completion in the individual experience of the entity.

This is the influence also, or the activities spoken of [in Joel 2:28], as the door upon and through which the old men may dream dreams, the young men may see visions. 281-58

As this center becomes more and more purified, healing by the laying on of hands becomes possible. Healing through the power of the spoken word may also be effected, for this purification makes possible the fulfillment of an exalted purpose.

Jesus lifted the understanding of those in His day from despair to hope, from sin to holiness, from weakness to strength, from selfishness to selflessness and from darkness to light. Paul was lifted from darkness into the light of Truth. Peter, by His smile of forgiveness, was raised from cowardice to courage. Mary Magdalene, through the compassion of Jesus, was led from sin to salvation. The crippled man at the pool of Bethesda was made to face self by Jesus with the words, "Wilt thou be made whole?" followed by the benediction, "Rise, take up thy bed, and walk." (John 5:6, 8) The multitudes who heard Him were led from selfishness to attempt selflessness. The despair of Lazarus' family at his death was turned into joy and hope eternal.

What were His promises to all of us through the disciples? "Verily, verily, I say unto you, He that believeth on me, the works that I do shall he do also; and greater works than these shall he do; because I go unto my Father." (John 14:12)

It is through the pituitary that one may enter the very presence of God. One may sense His Presence first as an experience apart from self and then, with the merging of the "I am" within with the great "I Am That I Am," there comes the Oneness with God.

"If, therefore, thine eye be single, thy whole body shall be full of light." (Matt. 6:22) If the "I" that is our ideal is one with the "I Am That I Am," then indeed we may become a light on the path to Him. "If thine eye be evil, thy whole body shall be full of darkness." (Matt. 6:23) Hence, the need for ideals.

The readings indicate the following experience which is also a sign that we are making practical application of spiritual law.

. . . as the progress is made, as the understanding comes more and more; *never, NEVER* does it make the manifested individual entity other than the more humble, the more meek, the more long-suffering, the more patient. Of this ye may be sure. 281-31

A Moslem mystic of the 17th century, Tewekkul Beg, expressed it in this fashion: "Thou wert I, but dark was my heart; I knew not the secret transcendent."

Plotinus: "God is not external to anyone, but is present with all things, though they are ignorant that He is so."

Jesus: "I and my Father are one." (John 10:30)

St. Augustine: "I was swept up to Thee by Thy Beauty, and torn away from Thee by my own weight."

With the experience of the presence of God comes also a greater courage to remain "to thine own self true" in this world of bleak conformity.

Chapter Six

REWARDS OF MEDITATION

Meditation brings an increase in vigor and improved health. An expansion of consciousness is achieved, and with this expansion comes the realization that we are in eternity *now*.

The readings say that eternity is the realm of the righteous. From this we gather that eternity is a dimension, not of time but of grace. This cannot be wholly understood in this realm, any more than God can be wholly comprehended by a soul in its earthly state. But the soul *is* able to realize that it belongs to a much wider world than the one which it now inhabits.

A shifting of consciousness takes place from the material and selfish to the non-material and selfless. There comes also the consolation that God not only has faith in us, but that He can and does make use of us. Moreover, we receive more opportunities to serve as more and more we put to good use the knowledge we have gained. As a result of this, a fuller comprehension of the errors in self and the goodness in others is born, as increasingly His Spirit manifests in daily life. A deeper psychic sensitivity to the problems and needs of others enables us to be of greater service to our fellowmen.

Increased, too, are the opportunities to meet our own short-comings by stepping up the tempo of karmic repayment (debts or sins left over from other lives). This restitution sometimes takes the form referred to by the mystics as "the dark night of the soul." According to Evelyn Underhill, this experience comes in order that the soul may develop greater virtues. This also explains why, when a soul has become seriously determined to better itself, problems seem to multiply.

This should make it easier to understand Edgar Cayce when he replied to questions about the process of healing:

Here, let's analyze healing for the moment, to those that must consciously —

30

as this body — see and reason, see a material demonstration, *occasionally* at least! Each atomic force of a physical body is made up of its units of positive and negative forces, that brings it into a *material* plane. These are of the ether, or atomic forces, being electrical in nature as they enter into a material basis, or become *matter* in its ability to take on or throw off. So, as a *group* may raise the atomic vibrations that make for those positive forces as bring divine forces in action into a material plane, those that are destructive are broken down by the raising of that vibration! That's *material*, see? This is *done* through *Creative* Forces, which are God in manifestation! Hence, as self brings those *little* things necessary, as each is found to be necessary, for position, posture, time, period, place, name, understanding, *study* each, and assist each in their respective sphere. So does the *entity become* the healer . . .

. . . there must be raised in each individual that consciousness of the indwelling, or — to put it in material manner — the *superseding* of the Christ Consciousness *in* that matter that would be healed, whether by its injection by those that through cooperation raise such vibrations in an individual, or through that of one individual raising same in *self*. So, all these receive their consideration, as has been given — *to* whom ye speak, *how* ye speak, where, when, and *how* — these *must all be* considered, would one *not* become arrogant, would one *not* become self-centered, self-condemning. Self surrendering first, then raise the consciousness that will supersede, will overcome — for only in *His* name may the world and *its* environs be overcome; for, as *He* overcame even death, so may *ye* in *His* name overcome the ills that the flesh is heir to, through its advent into a material world. "I am *not* of this world. *Ye* are not of this world, if *ye* abide in me — but I may only be *manifest* in the material world through thine *own* raising of that consciousness. As I abide in the Father, and ye abide in me, *I* in ye, ye in me, we may bring that to pass *as* ye seek."   281-3

The realization dawns that indeed there is no death. The only real death is the separation in consciousness of the soul from God. When this has been overcome there is no death, for consciousness is continuous in whatever plane one manifests. "In my Father's house are many mansions; if it were not so, I would have told you. I go to prepare a place for you. And if I go and prepare a place for you, I will come again and receive you unto myself; that where I am there ye may be also. And whither I go, ye know, and the way ye know." (John 14:2-4)

Death of the physical body is no longer a terror to be feared, for it is but the passing of the soul into another dimension through another door, for further growth and development. Life and death have taken on their true meaning. Neither is to be feared; both offer a glorious opportunity to love and be loved.

It seems strange that Christianity, which teaches heaven hereafter, has so few Christians who want to go there. Death is delayed as long as possible, even at the cost of unbearable suffering. It is as if we *want* to believe, but cannot.

Through meditation, we may become aware of these other planes in dreams. Growing sensitivity enables us to meet occasionally with a loved one who, having passed on, no longer hopes for a life hereafter, but is enjoying it to the fullest.

This lends a deeper insight to the meaning of the words, "The Lord is my Shepherd." Which one of us has experienced God? Only when we have, can we say with David, "The Lord is my Shepherd." There is no worry or doubt, but serene inner tranquility. This is real faith, an inner knowledge of God, a reconciliation with Him.

"I shall not want." Can we say this with assurance? What did David mean when he said it? He knew that as long as he sought to obey the law he would never want for those things necessary to serve God. This does not ordinarily include such worldly luxuries as a mink or a Cadillac. Only that which will enable us to serve Him well is necessary.

We should place our trust in the Lord, then, knowing that He gives us all that is needed to fulfill our destiny. We each come into life with a job to do that no one else can do as well, if we seek the Lord. And we will discover our special job, if we but meditate, pray and serve.

"He maketh me to lie down in green pastures." Certainly the Lord gives rest to those who seek Him. For the promise has also been that He will not give us greater burdens than we can bear.

"He leadeth me beside the still waters." Even as sheep will not drink from turbulent waters, so does He lead us to the peaceful water of the life within. Meditation leads us to the water that refreshes us mentally, physically and spiritually, giving us peace.

"He restoreth my soul." Who but God can restore us to our rightful place beside Him? When? When each of us seeks Him with all his heart, mind and soul; then and only then can He guide us homeward. In all recorded history, we know of only one whose soul was fully restored to His side. This was Jesus, who became the Christ. He truly possessed His own soul, for He gained complete control of it. Having learned to control Himself, He was in complete control of the universe and its laws. He was not subject to the law of gravity, or any other law of nature. They became subject to Him. He stilled the storm. He walked on the water. He raised the dead. He healed the sick and cast out demons. He multiplied the loaves and fishes, and He walked away from their midst when they sought to push Him over the brow of the hill. (Luke 4:29-30)

He was precognitive about Himself and others. He was telepathic as He read the minds of the Pharisees. He was clairvoyant as He directed the fishermen where to cast their nets. He used the power of exorcism as he bade the possessing spirits to come out. He was all things to all men. And his admonition to us was, and is, "Be ye therefore perfect, even as your Father which is in heaven is perfect." (Matt. 6:48) Only then can our souls be restored to their rightful home.

"He leadeth me in the paths of righteousness for His name's sake." Nothing in itself is basically evil. It is the motive which makes a deed good or evil. If one is in doubt, he has but to turn to the life of Jesus and ask, "What would He have done?" Through meditation He becomes our guide. If by sharing His Spirit with us, He reveals to us our weaknesses, it is only to show us how to surmount them.

"Yea, though I walk through the valley of the shadow of death, I will fear no evil; for thou art with me." This promise is fulfilled as soon as we learn to seek Him in meditation. If God be with us, who or what can harm us? To lose the body is nothing. We have already discarded many, and feel no more concern for them now than we do for a pair of worn-out baby shoes.

"Thy rod and thy staff they comfort me." The "rod" is the adversity which the Lord permits to help strengthen our moral fiber. "For whom the Lord loveth He chasteneth." (Heb. 12:6) Only through adversities do we come to know our weaknesses and our strengths. False optimism leads us sadly astray more often than it tempers us. It is when we realize that "problems" are the kiss of God upon the soul, that we learn to be grateful for them. Being human, though, we are probably also glad when they are resolved.

The endocrine glands, as related to spiritual growth, form a symbolic staff — the pineal and pituitary representing the crook. The "staff" is the staff within. Nowhere does one receive more comfort than from within, where He dwells. When all earthly help fails, as it has a periodic habit of doing, He stands ready. If we are truly making an effort to obey His laws, we have but to seek, and we shall find Him. He will stay with us and work with us, guiding us in all things, as long as we keep trying. Only through us can the Kingdom of God come into the earth, led by the Christ Spirit. Works and faith are equally important in preparation for this.

"Thou preparest a table before me in the presence of mine enemies." The table, also, is within. It bears the sustenance of life that Jesus spoke of when He said, "I have meat to eat that ye know not of." (John 4:32) It is this spiritual force which sustains us constantly. Call it the hormones of the endocrine glands if you will, those hormones that bring health to the body, mind and spirit; names are only labels. What we think, eat and do, makes us what we are mentally, physically and spiritually.

"The presence of mine enemies." Who are our enemies? Our own selfish desires. All of them are waste products, dross from the lower four centers of the body, which are referred to as the four beasts in The Revelation (4:6-9). Zechariah envisioned them as chariots drawn by different colored horses (Zech. 6:1-7). They are symbolized as the "living creatures" in Ezekiel (1:4-17) and as the four horsemen of the Apocalypse (Rev. 6:2-8). These four lower centers are the gonads, the cells of Leydig, the adrenals and the thymus.

The statement that we are our own worst enemies has become a cliche, but it contains such truth that if it were universally understood it would change the nature of mankind.

"Thou anointest my head with oil; my cup runneth over." In the Old Testament there are frequent references to God's chosen being annointed with a holy oil, as was David by Samuel (Sam. 16:13). In the New Testament, annointing is symbolic of the action of the Holy Spirit. In I John 2:20 we read, "But ye have an unction from the Holy One, and ye know all things." The anointing of the "holy one" is the experience already referred to, relating to the pineal and pituitary glands. When the "bread and wine" are partaken of at the level of the pineal, true communion with His Spirit, the Holy Spirit, begins. It is only after the descent of the Holy Ghost that we experience the anointing until the "cup runneth over."

"Surely, goodness and mercy shall follow me all the days of my life." We know from the promises of Jesus that He ceaselessly guards, guides and protects His own, and those for whom they intercede. Who are His own? Those who throughout their lives attempt to aid the coming of His kingdom in the earth. All promises in the Bible are conditional; we have to do our part. Only then will an advancement be sanctified by Him. Thus we must believe, if we would have peace. Again, it is Jesus who set the pattern. When Pilate reminded Him that he had the power of life and death over Him, He answered: "Thou couldst have no power at all against me, except it were given thee from above." (John 19:11) When Jesus realized that He should subject Himself to death on the cross, He went willingly and gladly, with peace in His heart, commending His soul to God. He had to show man that his true self prevailed over hell, death and the grave. Without His death on the cross, man could never have comprehended the immortality of the soul.

"And I will dwell in the house of the Lord forever." Where is the house of the Lord? Jesus said, "In my Father's house are many mansions." These "mansions" of God, these "pillars in the temple" are levels of consciousness. Where is consciousness? Within the bodies we now occupy, wherever we are. "For ye are the temple of the living God; as God hath said, I will dwell in them, and walk in them, and I will be their God, and they shall be my people." (II Cor. 6:16)

Therefore, whether we are on this earth, or in another dimension, the "house of the Lord" is the shell which we occupy. If the body is in pain, if the mind is in torment, if the soul is without peace, then sin lies at the door. For while God wills that no soul shall perish, He will not force man to seek Him.

As E. Stanley Jones wrote, the purpose of religion is not so much to get us into heaven, or to keep us out of hell, but to put a little bit of heaven *into* us, and take the hell *out* of us. This has always been the greatest responsibility of the church. Surely, meditation is one of the direct approaches to this end.

Chapter Seven

DREAMS AND VISIONS
RESULTING FROM MEDITATION

The following questions asked of Edgar Cayce relate to the dreams, visions and experiences of the first study group which practiced meditation. They should prove helpful to the reader.

Q-5. In a vision I saw a loaf of whole-wheat bread. One end was cut off so that the cells in the bread were very prominent. A great light shone from within the bread, illuminating every cell and reflecting a very large aura which entirely surrounded the bread. Please interpret.

A-5. This, emblematical as understood, stands for the essence of life itself in its cell force, showing forth in its activity that of the radiant life of Him who gave, *'I am the bread of life; he that eateth me shall not hunger,'* and as is visioned, that each makes for its own radiation that, combined in one, gives that full illumined life that brings understanding, and retains and builds, and gives – *truly* – the life everlasting.

Q-18. Am I beginning to see auras?

A-18. As life, light and love – with understanding – is reflected in self, so may there be seen those of the same reflection from others.

Q-19. What is the significance of the flashes and forms which I frequently see?

A-19. Those of the higher vibrations of inter-between, as well as spiritual forces taking forms in or before the mental self.

Q-20. Should I develop automatic handwriting?

A-20. We would not advise it! Too easily is it misleading, especially when there are so many flashes about. Rather that of intuitive force that may be guided by higher sources. 281-4

Q-11. While meditating I have experienced a perfect relaxation of the body, the head being drawn backward. Please explain.

A-11. The nearer the body of an individual . . . draws to that attunement, or consciousness . . . as is in the Christ Consciousness, the nearer does the body . . . become a channel for life — *living life* — to others to whom the thought is directed. Hence, at such periods, these are the manifestations of the life, or the spirit, acting through the body.

Q-12. On several occasions while meditating with the group, there was a cool feeling as if mentholatum had been placed upon my head and forehead, extending down upon the nose.

A-12. As would be termed [literally] as the breath of an angel, or the breath of a master. As the body attunes self, as has been given, it may become a channel where there may be even instant healing with the laying on of hands. The more often this occurs, the more power is there felt in the body, the more forcefulness in the act or word.

Q-13. After meditating with the group on April 11th, my whole body seemed to be vibrating to the thought that I had opened my heart to the unseen forces that surround the throne of grace and beauty and might, and had thrown about self that protection that is found in the thoughts of Him. Please explain.

A-13. Just as has been given, the nearer one . . . draws to that complete consciousness that is in Him, the greater may be the power that is manifested through His presence in the world through that as is brought about in self's own experience; the more forceful, the more helpful does the body become at such, and through such, experiences. Let these remain as sacred experiences, gathering more and more of same — but as such is given out, so does it come.

A-14. How can I develop greater spiritual control over the mental body during meditations?

A-14. The more that there is held that the mental and physical body is surrounded by, is protected by, that consciousness of the Master that gave, *'I will not leave thee comfortless,'* and the greater the physical can be submerged, the greater will be the activity of the spiritual forces in and through such bodies.　　　　281-5

Q-4. What is the meaning of the dream I had in which I was handed a cup and spoon, and told to feed people with spiritual food?

A-4. As indicated, that it is necessary for much of that which may be given, or measured out, to be in small doses, and not in a manner that would cause the individuals to become antagonistic to that which would be as Truth. Know ye, no one finite mind may have all the Truth!　　　　281-6

Q-14. Please interpret the dream which I had on June 13, 1932

37

regarding the canaries which I healed. What relation to my work in the healing group?

A-14. As has been given, the body may raise itself to those influences where the healing may come even as spoken, or [by the] laying on of hands. As the chirping, or as the words of those that would twitter even as the canary that makes for those influences that would hinder, or cause those of fear, doubt to rise — these once rid in perfect understanding, and throwing aside doubt and all that would hinder, brings the closer walk with Him.   281-7

Q-24. I saw each one on the prayer list as notes in music. Through our attunement and their seeking, the Master Musician (Christ) began to play the notes, and harmony reigned throughout. I felt this was an illustration of vibrations in healing. Is this how the healing takes place?

A-24. Very beautiful illustration; but don't think it's all of it! No one mind may conceive all that may be done through the power of the Master Musician; for it may bud as the rose, it may be the song of the frog — or of any — even of those that would be, to self . . . grating vibrations; for the cricket on the hearth to self is obnoxious, but to some would bring harmony and peace, as home!
281-8

Q-10. Why am I told so often to "Be not afraid, it is I?"
A-10. For He will come to thee.

Q-11. Does this "I" mean my elder brother Jesus, and shall I not know Him when He appears to me?
A-11. Ye shall know Him, even as He knows thee; for He calls thee by name.

Q-12. Then, why should I be afraid?
A-12. For the doubt and the fear lie innate in self, and the warning is given that this not overcome thee.

Q-13. Have I been able to raise the Christ Consciousness in anyone?
A-13. Oft.

Q-14. Just how is it meant that I should keep in the attitude of listening?
A-14. Listening, even as they must have listened when He tarried in the Mount — and were afraid when He came to them walking, as it were, upon the water. As self then listens, knowing that — as the heart is right in Him — He may enter in.

Q-15. Just what method should I use in healing?
A-15. As has been given, and as has been the experience of self, in

raising the consciousness — in silence — of those whom the body or self would aid, even as it is done in self. As the experiences have been, so does the confidence grow in self in that direction. Confidence, then, is of the material or of the physical sense — while faith is an attribute of the soul and spiritual body.

Q-16. Can I use the method of laying on of hands?

A-16. This may be developed in self, even as the vibrations may be raised in self and in others. When there is that impelling force that arises to do, by word or by act, or by that raising in self, ACT in that direction and manner.

Q-17. How can I lose myself in giving life?

A-17. In becoming more and more conscious of that He gave in giving the promise to many. In giving more and more a unison of purpose in that thou doest and sayest day by day.   281-10

Q-6. What is the significance of the experience during my morning meditations in which I was asked my name three times, and after each I answered very emphatically, the third time so emphatically that it was heard by someone in the room. To whom was I talking?

A-6. As there has oft been the experience of individuals being called by the mentors, or those guards of the various forces as manifest in the material world; so may the call come to one who has set self in body-mind to serve, that is called to service. So, in the experience, the body consciousness was called by Him who would guide, direct; who is the Way, the Light that leads to the proper conception of relationships in the various elements and elementals of life itself. A call from Him, who called [to Martha] "Know ye not she [Mary] hath chosen the better part?"

Q-8. If during the healing meditations, the name of an individual starts a distinctive type of vibration, should one attempt to maintain this vibratory sensation during the whole of the meditation for that particular patient, or should there be some attempt made to raise such a sensation to a higher vibration such as from the backward and forward to the circular?

A-8. Raise same to the circular; for, as has been given, this becomes more of the universal type of transmission to those that would become sensitive to those vibrations being sent out.

Q-9. What vibratory sensation might one expect to follow the circular sensations?

A-9. As of passing into the presence of that which may materialize in voice, feeling, sight, consciousness of presence, and the like. Be not afraid, ever surrounding self with His presence of love;

for He has given His angels charge concerning thee, that they bear thee up, that thou stumblest not when thou wouldst aid.

Q-12. What is the cause of the sensation I feel in my eyes at times during meditation?

A-12. As is manifest by the activities of those that would bring healing to others, the healing of every sort must come first in self that it may be raised in another. This is the healing in self, with that raising of the vision that may heal in others.   281-12

Q-10. Please explain the experience I had several weeks ago, in a dream. I seemed to be passing through various experiences. Someone pierced a needle in my forehead, then there seemed to be darkness all around me. I began crying out, "My God, my God, where art thou?"

A-10. This is the body-consciousness experience (mentally and physically) of that through which the Master passed in the hour of trial on the Cross, and is a mental experience of the body or entity, or soul-body, which is developing . . . better ability for dissemination of the glory, the truth, the joy, the understanding that came with those experiences that are the awakening to greater abilities in anyone.   281-15

Here we have Edgar Cayce's answer to one who was sorely plagued with self-doubts.

Q-1. Is what is holding me back physical or laziness?

A-1. Rather that of indecision, incontriteness. Purge thy mind, thy body. Make thyself one with Him.

Q-2. Why do I not make a more continuous effort?

A-2. Is thy purpose a single one? — or art thou seeking — seeking without putting into practice that which thou knowest?

Q-3. In what way can I best serve while in this body?

A-3. Study to show thyself approved unto Him; not as an eye-servant, but as ye do it unto those in thine own house, as ye do it unto those that ye meet day by day; a smile, a cheery word, a hopefulness — optimistic, ever, in Him. For He is the way; He is the abundant supply — if ye but put thy trust in Him.

Q-4. How can I correct the condition which holds me back?

A-4. As has been indicated. Enter into thine inner chamber with thy Lord; meet Him there; seek and ye shall know. For He would speak with thee as thou wouldst with thy child. As thou as a mother lovest that which is of thee, of thine own body, of thine own blood, then knoweth thee not that as thou wouldst be gentle, as thou wouldst be patient, thy heavenly Father would be more patient with thee? Trust in Him; speak oft with Him.

Q-5. Why do I have a decided feeling against digging into the past?
A-5. Thou hast remembered well . . . Lot's wife! But rather know that what is necessary for thee will be given thee – of thy past, of thy present, of thy future. Are they not one in Him? He is from the foundation of the world . . . Lo, He is nigh unto thee!

Remember the vision thou art experiencing in the present. 922-1

[There is] a decided differentiation between that some people call destiny and that making self one with the Father; for while law is love, *love is law – and, as healing, is the contradiction of many man-made laws,* and in line . . . with laws that are universal; the last to be conquered is death itself . . . *He* is love. Hence this consciousness of His presence must be the basis of all healing . . . Ask only in His name believing, and it shall be done! 281-3

He that would know the way must be oft in prayer, joyous prayer, *knowing* He giveth life to as many as seek in sincerity to be the channel of blessing to someone . . . 281-12

Early in the morning call unto thy God, and in the evening forget not His love nor His benefits.

Then, at that period when ye each are first aware, as ye awake, be STILL a moment and know that the Lord is God. Ask that ye be guided, THIS day, to so live that ye may stand between the living and the dead.

In the evening as ye sit at meat, be STILL a moment. For there is greater power in being still before thy God than in much speaking. Again give thanks for the day and its opportunities. 281-60

To conclude this chapter on a personal note, the following is quoted from a letter written by Edgar Cayce, December 12, 1932: "Often have I felt, seen and heard the Master at hand. Just a few days ago I had an experience which I have not even told the folks here . . .

"The past week I have been quite 'out of the running,' but Wednesday afternoon, in my little office or den for the 4:15 meditation, as I knelt by my couch I had the following experience: First a light gradually filled the room with a golden glow that seemed to be very exhilarating, putting me in a buoyant state. I felt as if I were being given a healing. Then, as I was about to give the credit to members of our own group who meet at this hour for meditation (as I felt each and every one of them were praying for and with me), HE came. He stood before me for a few minutes in all the glory that He must have appeared in to the three on the Mount. Like yourself, I heard the voice of my Jesus say, 'Come unto me and rest!' "

Prayer and meditation bring all of us into this perfect relationship to the Light of the World, which first manifested when God said, "Let there be light!"

Let us seek this Light by becoming a light to others. As Jesus said, "Come unto me . . . take my yoke upon you, and learn of me." We come to Him through prayer and meditation. We take His yoke by yoking ourselves to others, in order to help them bear their loads. This makes every burden lighter to carry. As he took upon Himself the burdens of the world, so must we take upon ourselves the burdens closest to us, those of our neighbor, our community, our nation, if we are truly to become His disciples. Only then are we able to truly know Him and learn of Him for it is then that He and the Father abide with us.

Edgar Cayce has said that everyone of us must sometime, somewhere, learn to meditate. So why not *now*. The rewards are beyond measure, culminating in a glimpse of the glory that God has prepared for those who love His laws.

Chapter Eight
AN EDGAR CAYCE READING
ON MEDITATION

"In the minds of many there is little or no difference between meditation and prayer. And there are many gathered here who through their studies of various forms have very definite ideas as to meditation and prayer.

"There are others who care not whether there be such things as meditation, but depend upon someone else to do their thinking, or are satisfied to allow circumstance to take its course — and hope that sometime, somewhere, conditions and circumstances will adjust themselves to such a way that the best that may be will be their lot.

"Yet, to most of you, there must be something else — some desire, something that has prompted you in one manner or another to seek to be here now, that you may gather something from a word, from an act, that will either give thee hope or make thee better satisfied with thy present lot, or to *justify* thee in the course ye now pursue.

"To each of you, then, we would give a word:

"Ye all find yourselves confused at times, respecting from whence ye came and whither ye goeth. Ye find yourselves with bodies, with minds — not all beautiful, not all clean, not all pure in thine own sight or in thy neighbor's. And there are many who care more for the outward appearance than that which prompts the heart in its activity or in its seeking.

"But, ye ask, what has this to do with Meditation? What *is* meditation?

"It is not musing, not daydreaming; but as ye find your bodies made up of the physical, mental and spiritual, it is the attuning of the mental body and the physical body to [their] spiritual source.

"Many say that ye have no consciousness of having a soul — yet the very fact that ye hope, that ye have a desire for better things; the very fact that ye are able to be sorry or glad; indicates an activity of the mind that takes hold upon something that is not temporal in its nature — something that passeth not away with the last breath that is

43

drawn, but takes hold upon the very source of its beginning – the *soul* – that which was made in the image of thy Maker – not thy body, no – not thy mind, but thy *soul* was in the image of thy Creator.

"Then, it is the attuning of the physical and mental attributes seeking to know the relationships to the Maker. *That* is true meditation.

"How do you accomplish same? How would ye as an individual go about learning to meditate?

"For ye must learn to meditate just as ye have learned to walk; to talk; to do any of the physical attributes of thy mind [with relation to] the facts, the attitudes, the conditions, the environs of thy daily surroundings.

"Then there must be a conscious contact between that which is a part of the body-physical, thy body-mental, to thy soul-body, or thy super-consciousness. The names indicate that ye have given these metes and bounds, while the soul is boundless – and is represented by many means or measures or manners in the expressions in the mind of each of you.

"But there are physical contacts which the anatomist finds not, or those who would look for imaginations or the minds. Yet it is found that within the body there are channels, there are ducts, there are glands, there are activities that perform no-one-knows-what – in a living, *moving,* thinking being. In many individuals such become dormant. Many have become atrophied. Why? Non-usage! Non-activity! Because only the desires of the appetite, self-indulgences and such, have so glossed over or used up the abilities in these directions, that they become only wastes, as it were, in the spiritual life of an individual who has so abused or misused those abilities that have been given him for the greater activity.

"Then purify thy mind if ye would meditate. How? Depending on what is thy concept of purification! Does it mean to thee a mixing up a lot of other things; or the setting aside of self, a washing with water, a cleansing or purifying by fire, or what not?

"Whatever thy concept is, be *true* to thine inner self. *Live* that choice ye make – *do it!* Not merely say it, but *do it!*

"Purify thy body. Shut thyself away from the cares of the world. Think on those things ye would do to have thy God meet thee face to face. 'Ah,' ye say, 'but many are not able to speak to God!' Many, ye say, are fearful. Why? Have ye gone so far astray that ye cannot approach Him who is all-merciful? He knows thy desires and thy needs, and can only supply according to the purposes that ye would perform within thine own self.

44

"Then, purify thy body physically. Sanctify thy body, as the laws were given of old, for tomorrow the Lord would speak with thee – as a father speaketh to his children. Has God changed? Have ye wandered so far away? Know ye not that as He has given, 'If ye will be my children, I will be thy God' and 'Though ye wander far away, if ye will but call, I will hear'?

"If any of you say, 'Yes, but it was spoken to those of old – we have no part in such,' then indeed ye have no part! They that would know God, would know their own souls, would know how to meditate or to talk with God, must believe that He *is* – and that He rewards those who seek to know and to do His biddings.

"That He gave of old is as new today as it was in the beginning of man's . . . seeking to know the will of God, if ye will but call on Him *within* thine inner *self!* Know that thy body is the temple of the living God. *There* He has promised to meet thee!

"Are ye afraid? Are ye ashamed? Have ye so belittled thy opportunities, have ye so defamed thine own body and thine own mind that ye are ashamed to have thy God meet thee within thine own tabernacle?

"Then, woe be unto thee lest ye set thy house in order. For as has been indicated, there are physical contacts in thine own body with thine own soul, thine own mind. Does anyone have to indicate to you that if you touch a needle, pain will be felt? Ye are told that such an awareness is an activity of consciousness that passes along the nervous system to and from the brain. Then just the same there are contacts with that which is eternal within thy physical body. For there is the bowl that must one day be broken, the cord that must one day be severed from thine own physical body – and to be absent from the body is to be present with God.

"What is thy God? Are thine ambitions only set in whether ye shall eat tomorrow, or as to wherewithal ye shall be clothed? Ye of little faith, ye of little hope, that allow such to become the paramount issues in thine own consciousness! Know ye not that ye are His? For ye are of His making! He hath willed that ye shall not perish, but hath left it *with thee* as to whether ye become even aware of thy relationships with Him or not. In thine own house, in thine own body, *there* are the means for the approach – through the desire first to know Him; putting that desire into activity by purging the body, the mind of those things that ye know, or even conceive of, as being hindrances – not what someone else says! It isn't what you want someone else to give! As Moses gave of old, it isn't who will descend from heaven to bring you a message, nor who would come from over the seas, but lo, ye find Him within thine own heart, within thine own consciousness; if ye will but *meditate,* open thy heart, thy mind! Let thy body and mind be channels that *ye* may *do* the things ye ask God to do for you! Thus ye come to know Him.

"Would ye ask God to do for ye that which ye would not do for your brother? If ye would, ye are selfish and know not God! For as ye do it unto the least of thy brethren, ye do it unto thy Maker. These are not mere words — they are that as ye will *experience* if ye would know Him at all. For He is not past finding out; if ye will know Him, tune in to Him. Turn, look, hope, act in such a way that ye *expect* Him, thy God, to meet thee face to face. 'Be not afraid, it is I,' saith He that came to those seeking to know their relationship with their Maker. And because He came walking in the night, in the darkness, even upon the waters, they were afraid. Yea, many of you become afraid, because of the things that ye hear — for ye say, 'I do not *understand* — I do not *comprehend*!' WHY? Have ye so belittled thyself, thy body, thy mind, thy consciousness, that . . . thou hast made of [no] effect those opportunities within thine own consciousness to know thy Maker?

"Then to all of you:

"Purify thy body, thy mind. Consecrate thyselves in prayer, yes — but not as he prayed: 'I thank Thee I am not like other fellows!' Rather let there be in thy heart that humbleness — for ye must humble thyself if ye would know Him — and come with an open, seeking, contrite heart, desirous of having the way shown to thee.

"And when thou art shown, turn not thy face the other way; but be true to that vision that is given thee. And He will speak, for His promise has been, 'When ye call I will hear, and will answer speedily.' Then, when He speaks, open thy heart, thy mind to . . . the glories that are thine — if ye will but accept them through that attuning, through meditation of thy consciousness, thy desire to know the *living* God; and say and live within thyself as He of old gave, 'Others may do as they may, but as for me, I will worship — yea, I will serve the living God.'

"He is not far from thee! He is closer than thy right hand. He standeth at the door of thy heart! Will ye bid Him enter? or will ye turn away?"   281-41

Chapter Nine

EFFECTIVE PRAYER

Meditation does not lessen the need for prayer, because it does not take the place of prayer. Prayer is a mental activity on our part addressed to God. Meditation is a listening state so that we may hear God speak to us.

Prayer comes before meditation, before the affirmation; and we may pray, if need be, all day long as we go about our daily work. Jesus found it necessary at times to pray for long periods. Certainly prayer should be a constant activity of the religious heart.

The readings of Edgar Cayce remind us that "he that would know the way must be oft in prayer."

IS THERE MORE THAN ONE KIND OF PRAYER?

There are many types of prayer. Unfortunately the most common one is the "gimme" prayer, wherein we beg God for favors. Is this wrong? Not for some people. For prayer, the art of prayer, is an ever-growing experience. When there is an acceptance of God's presence, one knows that He will supply all that is truly needed to fulfill one's purpose in life.

The art of visualization, so common today as a form of prayer, is another type of the "gimme" prayer. We want to make sure that He knows exactly what we want, so we send Him "pictures" of it. If we are going to tell God that we know what is best for ourselves what is the point in praying in the first place?

Jesus prayed, "Not my will, but Thine be done." The enlightened soul relegates the "gimme" prayer to the nursery toy box, and turns to the prayer of thanksgiving, of adoration, of petition for the woes of others, always adding, "Thy will be done."

The readings tell us that the daily prayer of Jesus was, "Others, Lord, others." From this it is self-evident that the prayers of supplication of the awakened soul deal primarily with the needs of others. The more we pray for others, the more we gain in the power to pray, and the more are we ourselves blessed. For how can we sincerely pray for another, and not be praying for ourselves, too?

Even the prayer "Be merciful to me, a sinner," while necessary in the early stages for some, is for others a mere indulging of the ego. However, it is as effective a prayer as any for those who need proof of His forgiveness before they can accept it. We should be aware, though, that if our concern lies in being merciful to others, we can take for granted His mercy to us. It is already ours. Indeed, as He is the very essence of mercy, it is obvious that He is always merciful to us.

Asking God for forgiveness shows proper repentance for wrongs committed, but unless those wrongs are righted by our own conscious effort, we shall never feel forgiven.

Repentance and confession in themselves cannot "purchase" full forgiveness. We must make amends as far as it is humanly possible. We must try to invoke the strength, through meditation, never to repeat the same error. If the guilt lies in the past, if the person whom we have harmed has already passed on, we can still project our prayer to where he is. The knowledge that we shall meet again all those with whom we have associated in the past should be of comfort in itself, in that we shall be given another chance to make amends.

God's forgiveness is a foregone conclusion, once we have turned from the shadows of sin to the light, once we have made every reasonable effort to rectify the wrong. This enables us not only to feel forgiven, but to erase the debt forever.

We may pray for guidance, but if we are not trying to do what we think is right, will He hear us? Yes, but we may not hear Him. As the Bible tells us, an unrepented sin seals our ears to the voice of God.

May we pray to escape further trials and tribulations? Certainly. Jesus did; but when He knew that He had to die on the cross to fulfill His purpose, He accepted it unfalteringly.

God does not wish to see us suffer; our adversities are of our own creation. We have erred in a sin either of commission or of omission, something we should not have done, or something we should have done. Just as a parent punishes a child in order to correct it, so the laws of God prove immovable when we try to resist them. The more we struggle to resist, the more hopelessly do we entangle ourselves at the mental or physical or material or emotional level, and sometimes on all four levels simultaneously.

Our attitude when we are sick or suffering should be, again, "Thy will be done." This calls for an inner submission while awaiting recovery, but doesn't stop us from doing all within our power to get

48

well. A rededication of heart and mind and an acceptance of suffering as a needed lesson have on more than one occasion brought instantaneous healing.

"Thy Will, *Thy* Spirit, *Thy* Ways" is the cry of the awakened soul.

HOW TO PRAY

Just as the disciples asked Jesus to teach them how to pray, so many people today ask the same question; it would be presumptuous of us, however, to tell another exactly how he should formulate the words of anything so personal and private as a prayer.

The words themselves are not important. It is the spirit in which they are said which is all-important.

God already knows more about the contents of our hearts than we do; our real need is to be perpetually aware of Him as the source of our protection, and so we pray to keep unbroken contact with Him. The words in themselves are not as important as some people would have us think. A story told by Edgar Cayce illustrates a beautifully direct approach to God by a very simple and earnest soul.

During his visits to the inmates of a local prison, Edgar Cayce used to teach a young boy about the kindliness of Jesus, explaining how He came to save us all. One day he arrived at the boy's cell and found him on his knees, his eyes closed and his hands tightly folded, intently repeating the entire alphabet from beginning to end. When he eventually ran out of breath and opened his eyes, the mystified Edgar Cayce asked him: "Son, what in the world were you doing?" The boy answered, "If that man Jesus is as wise as you say He is, He knows better than me what I'm trying to tell Him!"

Oh, that we might pray more often in that spirit! As Kahlil Gibran says, "God listens not to your words save when He utters them through your lips."

POSITIONS IN PRAYER

What is the best position in which to pray? A group of ministers once met to decide that very problem. They talked at length without reaching any conclusion. Some insisted that it was essential to kneel. Those with bony knees said that it was just as effective to keep seated. Others felt that they had to pace to and fro to generate the necessary fire. When the debate threatened to become heated, they decided to leave the decision to the only parson who had been silent throughout. He came from a rural parish, and he answered them thus: "One day when I was late for service, I ran across a neighbor's yard and fell headlong into his well. Half way down, my foot caught in a broken board, and I hung there upside down. Brethren, I have never prayed so well before or since!"

49

I hope that proves that it is not our position but our sincerity which makes our prayers effective.

VOCAL OR SILENT

Should we pray aloud or silently? This depends on the individual. We must discover for ourselves which method puts us in closer relationship to God. For some, the silent prayer is more powerful; for others the spoken word seems to carry more conviction. We may find that sometimes one is more effective than the other, depending on the conditions governing our need to pray.

LONG OR SHORT

Should we pray long prayers or short ones? This depends on the occasion. Perhaps the dearest prayer to God is an ardent, "Thank you, Father, thank you."

An anxious prayer of love and concern for an ailing friend sometimes is most effective when the cry from the soul is no more than, "Help him, Father, help him!" The intensity of love behind such a prayer is transformed by God into healing energy.

A casual prayer does little. We must really care. When we pray for someone we love, deep sincerity and concern are manifested; and one way to stimulate this same concern for someone less close to us is to realize that even a complete stranger is very dear to someone.

Q-3. How do we know when to help an individual?

A-3. Do with thy might what thy hands, hearts, minds, souls, find to do, leaving the increase, the benefits, in *His* hands, who is the Giver of all good and perfect gifts. Be not faint-hearted because, as thou seest, it is not accomplished in the moment. What is eternity to a single experience? "No good thought shall return to me empty handed." Believest thou? Then thou knowest that which is given out *must* return full measure . . .

Keep that consciousness that in Him all things are done well. That that is not understood, trust — knowing that there will come the understanding as the awakening to the various laws of love that constitute life in its essence and development through the physical, material, mental and spiritual planes. 281-4

GROUP PRAYER

Should we pray alone, or ask others to pray with us? Most certainly there is power in numbers. Jesus, our example in all things, asked others to pray with Him. If the power of prayer is effective with only one person praying, know that it is magnified when many pray. The prayer of many, say the readings, is like a strong cord made up of the many threads of individual prayers, thus strengthening its power.

THE POWER OF PRAYER

Prayer directs the consciousness to God.

Through prayer, we solicit aid from divine power.

Prayer encourages humility.

Prayer takes one outside of self to Him.

Prayer brings guidance.

Prayer releases tensions.

Prayer brings healing.

Many people go into a state of meditation without realizing it when, worn out from prayer, they wait for answering help. Here the results of prayer are one with the rewards of meditation.

While we need always to call on the Lord, we need even more to listen to Him, and it is in the quiet of meditation that there is a stepping-up of spiritual receptivity in every phase of our being.

We learn so much more by listening. This is what the Bible means when it says: "Be still, and know that I am God." (Psalm 46:10)

Every religion speaks of the quest of the soul for the Holy Grail, the place of the Most High, the Light, the Father. The Chinese speak of it as "The Old Road"; the Hindus call it "The Path of Return"; and in Christianity it is referred to as the way back to the Father. Meditation is the gateway that leads us to Him.

AFFIRMATIONS
General

1. Lord, use me in whatever way or manner that my body may be as a living example of Thy love to the brethren of our Lord.
2. Be still, and know that I am God.
3. May there come into my consciousness more and more the love of the Father, through the Son, day by day.
4. May the words of my mouth and the meditations of my heart be such, O Lord, as to bring in my experience that Thou seest I have need of at this time.
5. Father, in Thy mercy, in Thy grace, bring to me and my consciousness the awareness of the peace of the Christ: that I may say the more and more, "Father, Thy will be done in and through me day by day."
6. Let the love of the Father make me more patient with my fellow man.
7. May the knowledge of the Lord so fill my life, my body, as to make of me a channel in His name.

For Healing

1. May the abundance of the Christ love fill my mind, soul, and body with the love that brings healing in every manner.
2. There is being created in my body that divine love of the Christ Consciousness that will eradicate all uncommon, or any, desires that would hinder the body from being physically fit.
3. Be Thou merciful, O Father, in the hours of need for my body, my mind, my soul. Heal Thou my every weakness through the Christ that makes me alive in Thee.
4. Keep me in the way, O Lord, that will bring healing, understanding, and a righteous heart in all my days.

For those lending themselves as channels for healing.

1. Our Father Who art in heaven, hear our pleading for Thy children, who in weakness have erred, and seek Thy face. Mercy, O God, to us all, through Him who promised what we ask in His Name will be done in these bodies.

2. May there be magnified in these bodies that the Father seest they have need of! Thy will, O Father, be done in these bodies, as thou seest they have need of.

3. There is being created that within the physical being that will bring such Christ Consciousness as to eradicate all disorder.

Consult *A Search for God,* Books I and II, and *That Ye May Heal* for other affirmations.

DISCOVER HOW THE EDGAR CAYCE MATERIAL CAN HELP YOU!

The Association for Research and Enlightenment, Inc. (A.R.E.®), was founded in 1931 by Edgar Cayce. Its international headquarters are in Virginia Beach, Virginia, where thousands of visitors come year round. Many more are helped and inspired by A.R.E.'s local activities in their own hometowns or by contact via mail (and now the Internet!) with A.R.E. headquarters.

People from all walks of life, all around the world, have discovered meaningful and life-transforming insights in the A.R.E. programs and materials, which focus on such areas as holistic health, dreams, family life, finding your best vocation, reincarnation, ESP, meditation, personal spirituality, and soul growth in small-group settings. Call us today on our toll-free number

1-800-333-4499

or

Explore our electronic visitor's center on the
INTERNET: http://www.are-cayce.com

We'll be happy to tell you more about how the work of the A.R.E. can help you!

A.R.E.
67th Street and Atlantic Avenue
P.O. Box 595
Virginia Beach, VA 23451-0595